FOREX FOR BEGINNERS

Day Trading Strategies to Make Money
Online With the 1-Hour Trade

TODD WILLIAMS

Contents

Forex For Beginners

Day Trading Strategies to Make Money Online With the 1-Hour Trade

Todd Williams

Introduction

Yes, Currency/Forex trading can be confusing and often times frustrating – especially when starting out. Therefore, I designed this to be a very clear and simple to follow Forex trading strategy guide to get you started achieving consistent profits day after day.

This book is easy to understand and to put in practice. It has very well defined entry, stop loss and exit levels. It teaches you how to construct a profitable forex trading system for yourself and how to avoid trading and money management mistakes.

Both beginner traders and more experienced traders that have not found a clear strategy to make profits consistently will find this book helpful.

Let's begin!

The Forex Market

In this chapter, you will learn:

- The basics of the forex market
- Speculating in the forex market
- The trading currencies
- Currencies in relation to other financial markets

THE BASICS of the Forex Market

EVERYONE KNOWS that the most traded financial market in the world is the foreign exchange market (forex market, sometimes known as FX market). The forex market is the center of world capital, over which lies the interconnection and movement of each country's capital and investment funds. For instance, an Asian speculative fund investing in Austria's Treasury bonds, or a Japanese financial company devoting some of its assets to the

Argentina stock exchange, each of these international transactions is made possible through the forex market.

The forex market is open round the clock, six days a week. It enables forex traders to trade positions at whatever time they please or act on events and news, as they happen. In this market, large funded trades as high as a billion dollars can be transacted in a matter of seconds. According to statistics, average daily currency trading volume is above the $2 trillion mark per day. To illustrate the idea, the average daily forex trading volume is about 15 times the size of the world's equity markets. Hence, the forex market is basically a trader's market.

Speculating in the Forex Market

The large part of currency trading volume is based on speculation, as opposed to commercial and financial transactions. Speculation means that forex traders buy and sell foreign exchange positions for short term profits based on a day to day, hour to hour, or minute to minute fluctuation of prices.

The biggest contributor of currency trading volume, as much as 75 %, is the major currencies. The major currencies represent the wealthiest and most developed economies.

You might ask, what is the factor that contributes to the efficiency and ease of buying and selling securities, stocks, financial instruments, and assets such as forex? That factor is liquidity. This refers to the overall level of market interest, or the level of buying and selling volume in the market at any point of time for a particular security, stock, financial instrument or asset. Simply put, the higher the level of liquidity, the deeper the market. The deeper the market, the level of efficiency and ease of buying and selling becomes higher.

Liquidity is an important factor since it measures how fast prices move between trade transactions over time. A highly liquid market can determine large trading volume transacted with minor changes in the price. Conversely, an illiquid market determines the prices as they move rapidly on lower trading volumes.

THE TRADING CURRENCIES

DEPENDING ON THE TIME ZONE, global financial centers such as London, Sydney and Tokyo are open at any given time. Moreover, currency or forex trading doesn't even halt its operations for holidays. This means that the forex market is open and active 24 hours a day, 7 days a week.

With respect to forex trading in the Asia Pacific Region, the financial trading centers are Singapore, Hong Kong, Sydney and Tokyo. It is important to note that most of the transactions in this region are focused on the Japanese Yen currency pairs.

With respect to forex trading in the European Region, it is important to note that most of the transactions in this area are focused on the European currencies and the Euro cross-currency pairs.

With respect to forex trading in the North American Region, it is important to note that on most days, market interest rates and market liquidity decrease significantly in New York during afternoons. On relatively less active trading days, the lower market interest results in stagnant prices. But on relatively more active trading days, the lower level of liquidity can trigger price movements. Traders also need to consider that lower levels of liquidity tend to prevail.

Currencies in Relation to Other Financial Markets

FIRST AND FOREMOST, always remember that the various financial markets are markets of their own. This means that they function in accordance with their internal dynamics, which is based on empirical date, positions of large financial institutions, global news and general market sentiment. However, markets sometimes display degrees of correlation with each other. Hence, it is imperative for a forex trader to consider each market as one unique market, a market of its own kind, and to trade between them individually.

The relationship of forex with gold over the long term is mostly inverse, with a weaker currency most likely resulting to a higher price of gold, and a stronger currency most likely resulting to a lower price of gold. However, in the short term, each market has its own movements, fluctuations, dynamics and liquidity.

The relationship of forex with oil is in conformity with the overall economic conditions of a financial district. For example, a high price of oil results to higher levels of inflation. And the higher the levels of inflation, the slower the economy's growth prospects. Conversely, a low price of oil results to lower levels of inflation. And the lower the levels of inflation, the faster the economy's growth prospects.

The forex markets and the equity markets only occasionally intersect so there is not much empirical evidence that can lead to a correlation between the two financial markets. One example of the two financial markets intersecting is when a stock market reaches extraordinary levels of volatility and fluctuations, the currency experiences more pressure.

The relationship of forex with bonds is intuitive because these two are both affected by expectations of interest rates by the stakeholders. There are times, however that the reaction of the forex market moves faster compared to that of bonds. At other times, the reverse happens. That is, the reaction of bonds moves faster than that of the forex market. As currency traders, you need to always be aware of the yield levels of the government bonds of the major currency countries. The purpose of this is to make sure that the expectations of the interest rate market are properly determined by the currency trader himself since changes in interest rates influence forex markets.

3

Forex Trading – The Mechanics

In this chapter, you will learn:

- How to buy and sell simultaneously
- The basics of currency pairs
- When to go long, when to go short
- How to calculate profit and loss
- How to read a forex price quote

HOW TO BUY and Sell Simultaneously

ONE OF THE most pervasive concepts newbie forex traders fail to understand at the outset of their trading career is the idea that each forex trade comprises a simultaneous buy and sell.

To illustrate, let us say you are interested in purchasing shares of Berkshire Hathaway in the stock market. If you did purchase the shares you desire, you hope to see the price of the shares go up. And if the shares go up, you simply sell the shares to the stock market with a profit.

However, the same thing is not true in forex trading. The purchase of a currency will mean a simultaneous sale of another. This is what the term 'exchange' in foreign exchange means. Simply stated, if you purchase the dollar and you desire for it to go higher to profit, the question you need to ask is this: Higher against what currency?

To think about it using the ideas of the stock market to ease your understanding, when a trader buys shares of a stock, the truth of the matter is that the trader is selling cash (simultaneous buying of shares of stock and selling cash). Conversely, if that same trader sought to sell the shares of stock he previously bought, he is in effect buying cash (simultaneous selling of shares of stock and buying cash)

THE BASICS of Currency Pairs

TO MAKE the newbie forex trader understand the concept better, realize that forex markets refer to trading currencies by pairs. That is, the names of the different currencies involved are being exchanged against each other.

THE FREQUENTLY TRADED Major Currency Pairs

THIS INVOLVES the US dollar on one side of the deal, and another currency on the other. The International

Standardization Organization (ISO) designates codes for each of the major currency pairs. The table below enumerates the frequently traded major currency pairs, their ISO code, the countries involved, the long name, and nickname.

The Frequently Traded Major Currency Pairs
ISO Currency Pair Code
Countries Involved, respectively
Long Name
Nickname

USD/CHF
US and Switzerland
Dollar – Swiss
Swissy
NZD/USD
New Zealand and US
New Zealand – Dollar
Kiwi
EUR/USD
Eurozone and US
Euro – Dollar
NA
USD/JPY
US and Japan
Dollar – Yen
NA
GBP/USD
United Kingdom and US
Sterling – Dollar
Sterling / Cable
USD/CAD

US and Canada
Dollar – Canada
Loonie
AUD/USD
Australia and US
Australian – Dollar
Aussie / Oz

THE FREQUENTLY TRADED Major Cross Currency Pairs

CROSS-CURRENCY PAIR REFERS to any currency or foreign exchange pair that does not involve the US dollar. Crosses enable forex traders to directly target their buying and selling of currencies to specific individual currencies in order to take advantage of current events.

To illustrate, let us say your fundamental analysis of the Canadian dollar suggest that it is the worst prospect of all the currencies to buy at that point of time, because of terrible interest rates and economic outlook in the region. In order to take advantage of this current event, you will be looking to get out of the Canadian dollar, or in other words, to sell it.

The next question to ask is this, "Against what currency will I sell my Canadian dollars?" You immediately thought about Canada's big economic powerhouse neighbor, the United States of America. Upon further research and analysis, you found that the US dollar is no good either, that its economic prospects are the same and hence it is not much better than the Canadian dollar. By looking for countries with high interest rates and strong economic growth prospects, you found the Japanese Yen.

In this instance, since your research and analysis tells you that the Canadian dollar has the worst prospect while the Japanese yen has the best, you would be looking to buy the JPY/CAD cross (buying Japanese yen while simultaneously selling Canadian dollar).

4

Currency Markets

The most actively traded major currency cross pairs have been highlighted in the table below.

The Frequently Traded Major Cross Currency Pairs
ISO Currency Pair Code
Countries Involved, Respectively
Market Name

AUD/JPY
Australia and Japan
Aussie – Yen
NZD/JPY
New Zealand and Japan
Kiwi – Yen
EUR/CHF
Eurozone and Switzerland
Euro – Swiss
GBP/JPY
United Kingdom and Japan
Sterling – Yen

EUR/JPY

Eurozone and Japan

Euro – Yen

EUR/GBP

Eurozone and United Kingdom

Euro - Sterling

WHEN TO GO LONG and When to Go Short

A LONG POSITION or simply termed as "long", refers to a market position in which a trader has purchased a security. In currency trading, this refers to having purchased a currency pair. Therefore, when you, the trader, are looking for prices to rise so you can sell the same at a higher price (preferably the peak price at any point of time) than you purchased it, you go long.

When you desire to close a long position, you are in effect intending to sell the currency pair that you earlier bought. And if you buy currency pairs at different levels of prices, you are in effect adding to longs or sometimes termed as "getting longer".

WHEN TO GO Short

A SHORT POSITION or simply termed as "short", refers to a market position in which a trader has sold a security that he never even owned. To illustrate this concept, let us say that you are a stock market or equity trader. If you, as an equity trader desire to short a stock, you are going to borrow a specific stock with specific number of shares so you can sell it.

However, in currency trading in the forex markets, this means that you as the trader have sold a currency pair. Having sold a currency pair means that you have sold the based currency in exchange for having bought the counter currency. Selling a currency pair, is called in the forex market as "going short" or "getting short". You profit in this scenario by watching out for the currency pair's price to diminish so you can take advantage of it by buying it back at a profit. If you as the forex trader sell at different price levels, you are adding to shorts and getting shorter.

SQUARING Up

Square or flat means that the forex trader has no position in the currency exchange market. Squaring up in currency trading means that the forex trader has an open position in the market, and currently looking to close it.

HOW TO CALCULATE Profit and Loss

MARGIN BALANCES and Liquidations

When you, as a newbie forex trader, open an online forex trading account, you will be required to provide some cash as collateral in order to support the margin requirements as established by individual foreign exchange trading brokers. Such initial cash deposit becomes the opening margin balance of a forex account and forms the basis of collateral of a trader's subsequent trade transactions.

To illustrate, let us say that your brokerage account requires a leverage of 100:1. This means that a $1 of margin can control a $100 position. Moreover, let us say that your broker requires a 100% margin ratio. This means that you have to maintain 100% of the required margin every time. Hence, to have a position size of $100,000, you have to shell out $1000 cash to your account as margin (1% of $100,000 is $100 as in the 100:1 ratio specified above).

The Difference between Unrealized and Realized Profits and Losses

ALMOST ALL OF the forex trading platforms around provide real-time mark to market calculations showing the margin balance of your account. "Mark to market" is the calculation that provides your unrealized profits and losses based on the positions you took on the forex market at any given time.

Realized profits and losses is what a forex trader gets when he intends to close out a position. If that trader did close out the full position, the profits or losses go into the marginal balance. Hence, if the trader closes out only the open positions, only that part will be deemed as realized as it goes to the margin balance.

If the trader has a winning position as open, the unrealized profits and losses is positive, and thus the margin balance rises. Conversely, if the trader has the market moving against his position, the unrealized profits and losses is negative, and thus the margin balance diminishes.

How to Calculate Profits and Losses through Pips

BASING on your position size and the number of pips you make or lose, the profits and losses calculations are easy to determine. A pip is the smallest increase or increment of fluctuations of price in the price of a currency. Among other traders, pips is also known as points. In this book, pips and points will be used interchangeably. Depending on the trading platform, most currency pairs are quoted using five digits. The last digit is the pip or point. Here are some examples with the pip underlined.

- USD/JPY: 123.2$\underline{1}$
- USD/CHF: 1.561$\underline{2}$

Looking at USD/JPY, if the price moves from 123.00 to 123.21, it has gone up by 21 pips or points. Conversely, if the price moves from 123.21 to 123.00, it has gone down by 21 pips or points.

In order to turn the pip movement into a profits and losses determination, you have to determine the size of the position. For example, for a 100,000 USD/JPY position, the 21-pip increase equates to 21,000 yen ($100,000 x .21 = 21,000 yen).

HOW TO READ a Forex Price Quote

BIDS AND OFFERS

When you, as the forex trader, are looking at a forex broker's online platform, you will see two sets of prices for each currency trading pair. The price on the left is the bid (this refers to the price at which you can sell the base currency at that given point in time) while the price on the right is the offer/ask (this refers to the price at which you can buy the base currency at that given point in time).

The price quotation of every bid and offer/ask has two

components. These are the big figure and the dealing price. The big figure is the first three digits of the overall currency rate while the dealing price is the last two digits of the overall currency price.

SPREADS

A spread is the difference between the bid price and the offer price. As most online forex broker trading platforms use this, look at spread as the compensation that the broker receives for executing your trade.

5

Forex Trading Strategies You Can Use

In this chapter, you will learn:

- Strategies used by professional forex traders
- How to apply the strategies in your trading career
- How to determine which strategies fit you
- How to develop market discipline

HOW TO FIND the Right Trading Strategy

A QUESTION that is always asked by newbie foreign exchange traders is, "What is the best and most profitable approach (technical analysis or fundamental analysis) or style (long term, medium term, or short term) to trade the forex market?" The truth is, there is no perfect and standard answer for this difficult question. The characteristics of forex trading market dictate that every approach is correct as it depends on the individual considerations and risk appetite of every forex market trader.

WORK AND LIFESTYLE Considerations

FIRST, think about the resources you have that are available to support your forex market trading. What are these resources? Time and money. Deciding how much of these two resources you have can help you determine how best to pursue your trading goals.

For instance, if you intend to be a full time trader, you have a lot of time to devote to forex market analysis and time devoted to actual forex market trading. However, if you have a full time job, your boss will not probably relish the fact that you use the time on the job to pursue your full time market trading. Hence, you can only trade and do market analysis during your free time. Be realistic.

When it comes to money, make sure that you do not risk capital that you need for the next 12 months or money you cannot afford to lose. The standard is, you only risk money that if lost, will not significantly affect your standard of living.

HOW TO MAKE Time for Forex Market Analysis

THE KEY to the success of every forex market trader is to develop an efficient and effective daily, weekly or monthly (as the case may be) schedule for forex market analysis. As a rule of thumb, your schedule must consist of the analysis of the following:

1. Regular updates of major market movements
2. Data releases and market events that will affect the forex market
3. Current events that include domestic and international politics, economics and public policy developments
4. Multiple time frame technical analysis of major currency pairs or at least your targeted currency pairs

CHOOSING between Technical and Fundamental Analysis

WHAT IS FUNDAMENTAL ANALYSIS?

FUNDAMENTALS ARE the economic fundamentals of a security or asset (country in the case of forex, stock in the case of the equity market) that are derived from the study of the news and information that reflect the macro-economic and political situations of the country whose currencies and money are being traded. The process of deriving the fundamentals from the news and information gathered is called fundamental analysis. Fundamentals of a country are usually on the levels of interest rates, the monetary policy of the country's government and central bank, economic data reports by the national economic authority of the country, international trade flows, and international investment flows.

What is Technical Analysis?

· · ·

TECHNICAL ANALYSIS IS a form of market analysis that more often than not includes charting analysis, mathematical and empirical studies of price sensitivity and behaviors, trend line analysis, and momentum or moving averages. Technical analysis can provide the trader some guidelines regarding how the prices of currency move, allowing him to predict the future direction of price changes.

Rather than choosing to use fundamental or technical analysis, it would be beneficial for a forex market trader, especially the new ones, to follow an approach that reconciles or combines the two. This will improve the forex market trader's chances of spotting trade opportunities and handling forex markets that are reacting to both fundamental and technical developments.

TERMS of Your Trading Activities

THE NEXT STEP is to settle on a trading style that fits the forex market trader. Most trading styles can be grouped into three main categories:

- Short term
- Medium term
- Long term

The truth is, styles overlap, and forex market traders can take advantage and adopt different styles for different forex market trade opportunities depending on the circumstances and their preferences. Hence, the goal of this book is to provide you basic information on each trading style so you can choose accordingly.

. . .

SHORT TERM FOREIGN Exchange Trading

SHORT TERM TRADING in the forex market is not the same as short term trading in other financial markets such as the stock market. This is because short term forex trading usually involves holding a sizable position for only a few minutes (sometimes even seconds) and rarely exceeding an hour.

The most important thing in short term forex market trading is the pip fluctuations. Short term forex market traders are seeking to profit handsomely by constantly and repetitively opening and closing positions after gaining just a few pips. Most of the time the target pips for short term traders is as little as 1 or 2.

Here are some important tips that will help you should you decide to follow a short term trading strategy in the forex market:

1. Trade only during times of peak liquidity and market interest
2. Focus on trading one currency pair at a time
3. Adjust your risk and reward expectations to reflect the spread

MEDIUM TERM FOREIGN Exchange Trading

THE MAIN IDEA of medium term foreign exchange trading

is determining where a forex currency pair is most likely to go (increase or decrease) or the direction it will likely take over the next several hours or days after opening the position and establishing a trading strategy to exploit the opportunity.

Although medium term foreign exchange traders are usually looking to profit from 50 to 100 pips over the next several hours or days after opening a position, they can also close the position for less than the targeted time as long as they capture at least 60-80% of the targeted pips. In other words, if after a couple of seconds or minutes the position already gained the 100 targeted pips, they will close the position out instead of waiting and holding the position and hoping it will still go higher over the targeted 1 day waiting period.

LONG TERM FOREIGN Exchange Trading

LONG TERM foreign exchange trading involves holding positions in longer time increments such as weeks, months and years. With proper management of risk, individual forex market traders can take advantage of long term trends. The most important thing is to make sure that you can withstand gains and losses in the short and long term (in other words, volatility and price fluctuations) of at least 5 – 10 %.

WHAT IS A CARRY TRADE STRATEGY?

TO PUT IT SIMPLY, a carry trade strategy is one when a

forex market trader purchases a high yielding currency and sells a lower yielding currency.

HOW TO DEVELOP a Disciplined Foreign Exchange Trading Plan

A TRADING PLAN is an organized way of executing a forex market trading strategy that a forex trader developed based on his outlook and analysis of the markets. The following are considerations you have to take when organizing a disciplined forex market trading plan:

1. Position size. Ask yourself how large a market position you are willing to take for each trade strategy.
2. Where should I enter the position determined?
3. It will be crucial to set stop loss and take profit levels in your trading plan.

THE IMPORTANCE of Taking Your Emotion Out Of Foreign Exchange Trading

THE TRUTH IS, you cannot block out emotions entirely. The best thing you can do is to understand the sources of your emotions, recognize them, and never letting them affect your trading. This is easier said than done. Below are a few tips to keep your emotions in check when trading forex:

1. Focus on the pips you gained, not on the money or cash.
2. Accept your losses from time to time. No one is a perfect trader.
3. It is not about having the correct and perfect trading style and strategy; it is about making money.

6

How to Start Trading Forex Today

In this chapter, you will learn:

- How to start your forex market trading through your practice account
- How to manage your trades
- How to evaluate the positions you took in consonance with the results

READY, Set, Click!

ALMOST EVERY FOREX broker offers newbies a free practice account. All you have to do is to sign up in the broker's website. Since it is funded with virtual money, you will be able to make your trades, practice your trading styles and strategies, and gain experience. This is the best course of action for the newbie forex market trader who wants to learn and experience the process up close and personal. However, one thing a practice account will not be able to simulate is the emotion of losing and gaining real money.

It is good to do your own research and read reviews regarding how satisfied others are with brokers. I've compiled a list of 5 of the most well-known Trading Websites to get started. However, again do your own research to eliminate risk and determine which broker is the best fit for you.

1. HTTP://WWW.OANDA.COM/ - Many traders believe has the highest profitability percentage. It does not require a minimum account deposit, which makes it easy to get started even if you have very little money to invest. It is a market maker broker meaning and you must do your own research to educate yourself on trades.

2. HTTP://WWW.ALPARI.COM/ - It has Online Forex Trades, as well as One-Click Trades; There are 2 Account types you can choose to sign up for- the Standard or the Pro. With the Pro, you get direct access to the Forex Market, giving you more ability to choose the options you want. This site includes a free research database; it has 24-hour support team that is multilingual. You also have the option to trade with a Forex Broker through this website.

3. HTTP://WWW.TRADEKING.COM - It requires $500 to start an account. Trades more than 45 currency pairs as well as gold and silver.

. . .

4. HTTP://WWW.ATCBROKERS.COM - This was founded in 2005 is for more experienced traders of Forex. It requires a large initial deposit.

5. HTTP://WWW.ETORO.COM/ - Known for its social network that is limited to traders, which can be very helpful for beginners. You are allowed to follow top traders and learn from others in the network. It also has a very low initial deposit amount. However, it does not include a metatrader software platform.

Go ahead and start your practice account with your chosen broker and get some practice!

CLICKING and Dealing

IN ORDER TO execute a planned trade on your practice account, specify the amount of the trade you desire to open and click on the buy or sell option on the trading platform to execute your trade. More often than not, the trading platform system responds within seconds.

7

How to Use Orders on the Trading Platform

Since the forex market is open for 24 hours a day, a market action is likely to happen even when you are not in front of the computer screen. Hence, orders will be a handy tool since these will enable you to act in the market without being in the market.

Professional and institutional forex market traders usually use orders to capture sharp and short term fluctuations in price, limit the volatility in an uncertain position, establish an entry and exit trade strategy, and maintain trading discipline.

DIFFERENT TYPES of Orders

- Take profit orders are used to lock in profits in an open position in the market. For instance, if you are short of USD/JPY at 116.10, your take profit order will be to purchase the position back and be placed below the short price, let's say at 110.6.

- Limit orders are orders that execute a trade at desired levels compared to the current market price. In the stock market and other financial markets, this is equivalent to the motto, "buy low and sell high". To illustrate, if your limit order is to sell the position, then the limit order must be placed at a price that is higher than the current market price. Conversely, if your limit order is to buy the position, then the limit order must be placed at a price that is lower than what is the current market price.

- Stop loss orders are orders that stop and limit your losses in the event that the forex market moves against your desired position. This is a very handy tool to limit your losses. Leaving everything to the market is dangerous.

- A trailing stop loss order is a kind of stop loss order that a forex market trader sets at a number of pips that is previously fixed from the entry rate in the position. This type of order adjusts the order rate as the level of market price moves; only in this case, it moves toward the direction of your trade.

- The OCO order is a kind of stop loss order but combined with a take profit order. In this order, the position that you took shall remain open until one of the order levels is reached by the foreign exchange market and thereby closing your position. When one order level is achieved (meaning the target pips you set were reached), the other order is automatically cancelled.

- Contingent orders are those that combine

several types of orders in order to establish a complete and comprehensive forex market trading strategy. Contingent orders are most commonly referred to as if/then orders.

MANAGE Your Trades

THE FOREX MARKET is not a wheel of fortune where you can simply place your bets with sure winnings, big or small. The forex market is dynamic and fluid; in a single blink of an eye, new information and prices develop thereby creating new opportunities for forex market traders and changing previous expectations.

The bottom line is this: a foreign exchange market trader can optimize his trading strategy by making sure that he thoroughly plans each trade before getting affected by his emotions. In this way, he can improve his overall chances of taking profits and gains while minimizing the risks and losses.

FOLLOW Current Events and Developments in Data and Information

IF YOU ARE FOLLOWING a medium to long term foreign exchange trading strategy, it would be best if you use wider take profit limits and stop loss orders. However, it would be a good idea if you stay on top of the market at all times, even if you are a long term forex market trader, since a lot can happen between the time you open and close a position. Unexpected events that can affect your positions may come at the most inopportune time.

A key point here: every forex market trading strategy needs to take into consideration future events, public policy, news, and other relevant data even before a position is opened. Hence, a prudent forex market trader will gather and take note of all the data and information available before he trades.

EVALUATE Your Trading Results

IN EVALUATING the outcome of any trade, it would be very beneficial if you look back over the whole process of opening and closing a position, as well as the time in between - regardless of the pips that you gained or lost. In this way, you will be able to understand what you did right and what you did wrong. Some key questions you can ask yourself are the following:

1. How did I identify the trading opportunity?
2. Did I take advantage of that trading opportunity?
3. What trading method did I use to gain the most pips or profits in a day or week or month or year?
4. How well did the original trading plan work out?
5. Was I able to monitor the market while my positions are open?

You have everything to gain and nothing to lose in this scenario. For instance, you can identify your good points and what you are not so good at, and adjust your forex market trading approach and methodologies accordingly. Evaluating your foreign exchange market trading results on a daily, weekly, monthly or yearly basis is a crucial step in improving your trading acumen and diminishing your trading losses.

CPSIA information can be obtained
at www.ICGtesting.com
Printed in the USA
LVHW080957201220
674416LV00013BA/1422